B is for Bagpipes

A Scotland Alphabet

Written by Eve Begley Kiehm and Illustrated by Alexa Rutherford

Dedicated with love to
My children and stepchildren
Juliet, Dermot, Randy, Darrell, Verity, Rhondda
and my grandchildren
Alida, Jenna, Kristen, Peyton, Kevin, Jack
—E. B. K.

✠

For Elliot—
My grandson living in the South of England,
to help him become a Scot. Also for my family,
Ross and Rowan, my mother, and
especially John for all his help.
—A. R.

Sleeping Bear Press™
2395 South Huron Parkway, Ste. 200
Ann Arbor, MI 48104
www.sleepingbearpress.com

Printed and bound in the United States.

10 9 8 7

Library of Congress Cataloging-in-Publication Data

Kiehm, Eve Begley, 1933-
B is for bagpipes : a Scotland alphabet / written by Eve Begley Kiehm; illustrated by Alexa Rutherford.
   p. cm.
ISBN 978-1-58536-453-4
1. Scotland—Juvenile literature. 2. English language—Alphabet—Juvenile literature. 3. Alphabet books. 4. Scotland—Juvenile poetry. I. Rutherford, Alexa, ill. II. Title.
DA762.K54 2010
941.1—dc22
2009036940

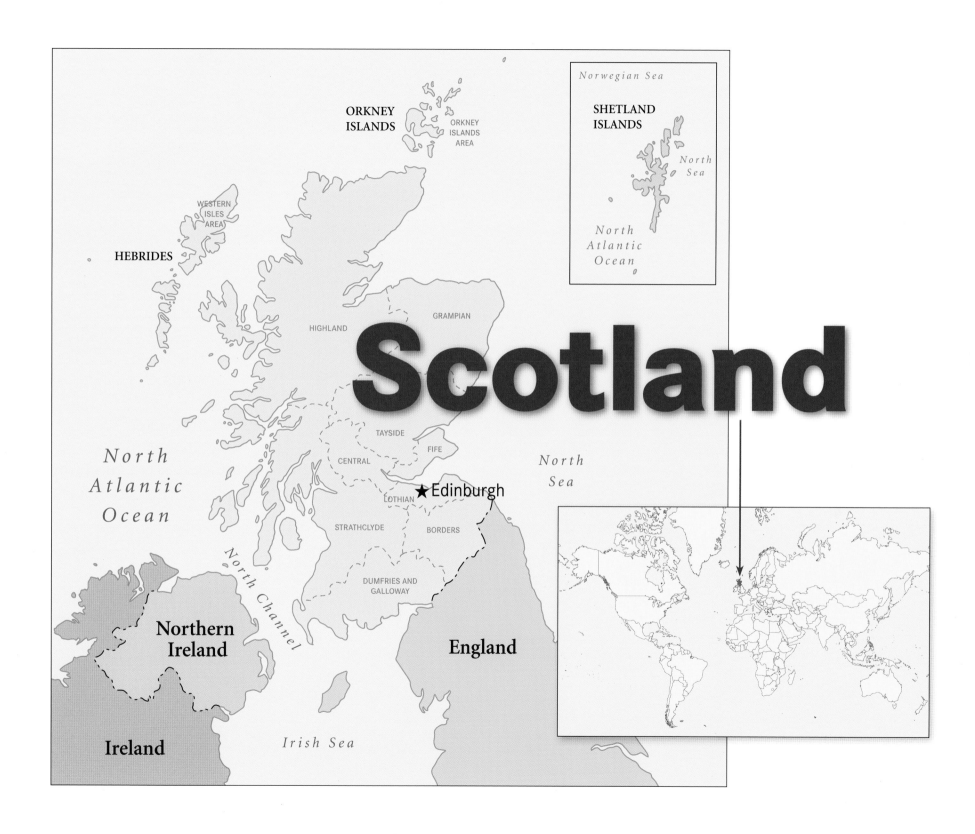

Scotland

ORKNEY ISLANDS

ORKNEY ISLANDS AREA

WESTERN ISLES AREA

HEBRIDES

Norwegian Sea

SHETLAND ISLANDS

North Sea

North Atlantic Ocean

HIGHLAND

GRAMPIAN

North Atlantic Ocean

TAYSIDE

CENTRAL

FIFE

North Sea

LOTHIAN

★Edinburgh

STRATHCLYDE

BORDERS

DUMFRIES AND GALLOWAY

Northern Ireland

North Channel

England

Ireland

Irish Sea

In Scotland, the week between Christmas and the New Year used to be called "the daft days" and was always a time for parties and fun. Hogmanay, a Scots word for New Year's Eve, finds Scots around the world linking crossed arms with family and friends and singing Auld Lang Syne. Set to a traditional melody, the words were written by poet Robert Burns, and the message is about old friendships and happy bygone days.

Every Scot who travels abroad carries with him or her a bit of the traditions of Scotland. So when the clock strikes twelve midnight on December 31st and everyone has sung Auld Lang Syne at least once, the custom of first-footing is often observed. This means that the first person crossing the doorstep after midnight is welcomed in—especially if the visitor is a dark-haired man carrying some food or drink and maybe a coin for luck. (Blonds are not so welcome because they are reminders of olden days when you might open your door to a Viking invader!) The first-footer is given a "Ne'erday" (New Year's) drink and perhaps a piece of short-bread or spicy fruitcake encased in pastry, known as blackbun.

A's for Auld Lang Syne
(long, long ago).
With memories of good times,
and memories of woe.

Should auld acquaintance be forgot,
And never brought to mind?
Should auld acquaintance be forgot,
And days of auld lang syne?
For auld lang syne, my dear,
For auld lang syne,
We'll tak' a cup o' kindness yet,
For auld lang syne.

B is for Bagpipes
sweet and wheezy.
Playing them
is never easy.

Bagpipes consist of an airbag (usually made of leather) and a number of pipes. To play, you blow into a pipe to fill the bag with air. Then you squeeze the bag under your arm, pushing the air out through the drone pipes (named for the "droning" or low humming sound they make), and the chanter, which has finger holes so you can play different notes. Bagpipes are not easy to play because you need to finger, blow hard, squeeze, and keep it all together at once.

In Scotland they cover the leather bag with a layer of tartan cloth. Scotland may not have invented the bagpipes, but if you see pipes with a tartan "bag" they are certainly Scottish. The Great Highland Bagpipe is most appreciated outdoors as it is—well, um—LOUD. Much pipe music was composed centuries ago and passed down unwritten. A true Scot is moved by the sight of a hundred pipers playing in tune marching down a green hillside to the strains of "Scotland the Brave."

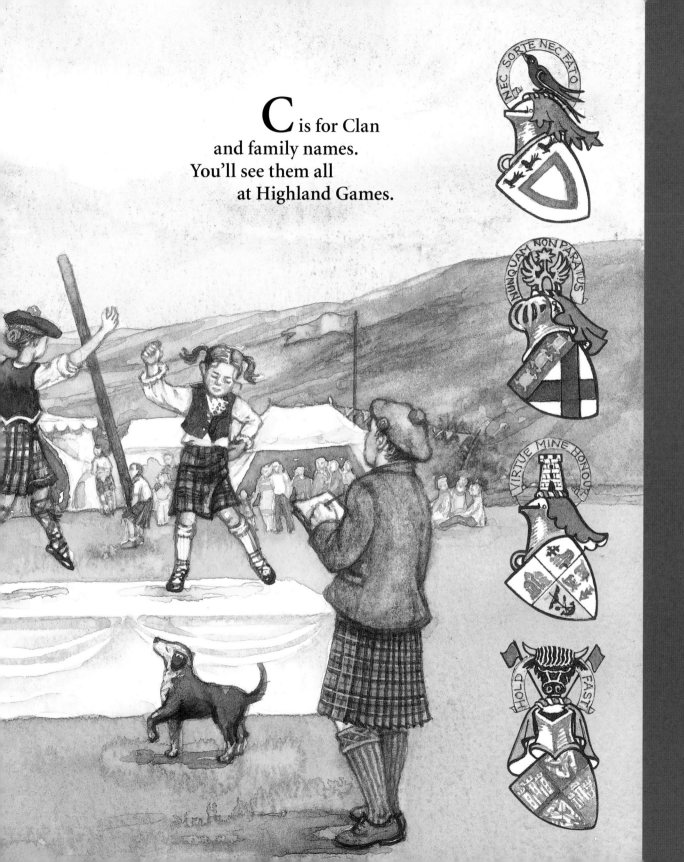

C is for Clan
and family names.
You'll see them all
at Highland Games.

The Gaelic word "clann" means children. To the old Scottish chieftain, his clan was his family and he was the father who provided for them and protected their interests. In return, they pledged their loyalty and support when their chieftain needed it, in battle or otherwise.

Many of the clan names start with either Mc or Mac, both syllables meaning "son of," so that the first Macdonald was the Son of Donald. The Vikings left us ancient names like MacLeod and McIver and the Normans and Flemish left names like Cameron and Fraser. The Highland clans were a proud bunch and there was a lot of in-fighting—we still use the adjective "clannish" to describe groups that stick to themselves. Clans were also common on the Scottish Borders where you will find Douglases, Maxwells, Johnstones, and others.

Some clans like to claim descent from Adam himself and there's a story about the MacLeods and the MacLeans arguing which clan was older. The MacLeod said, "Indeed, we never saw you on board Noah's Ark," to which the MacLean replied, "The MacLean had a boat of his own."

Traditional Scottish dancing has two distinct rhythms—the reel, which is quick, and the Strathspey, which is slow and stately. These are group dances, usually with four, six, or eight people forming a "set."

The most common dances in use today are the Dashing White Sergeant and the Eightsome Reel—and they will leave you breathless! You'll hear some loud "Hoochs" all around as the party warms up. A room of tartan-clad lads and lassies, the floor reverberating with many feet, the skirl of pipes or the rhythm of a fiddle, and an accordion band warm the cockles of a Scot's heart.

Young people still compete for honors in Highland Dancing with dances like the Highland Fling, the Sword Dance, and the Seann Triubhas (pronounced "sheen trews" and means "old trousers"). This dance was born when the law forbidding the wearing of the kilt was repealed. Now Scots could kick up their heels again and wear the kilt—freed from old trousers!

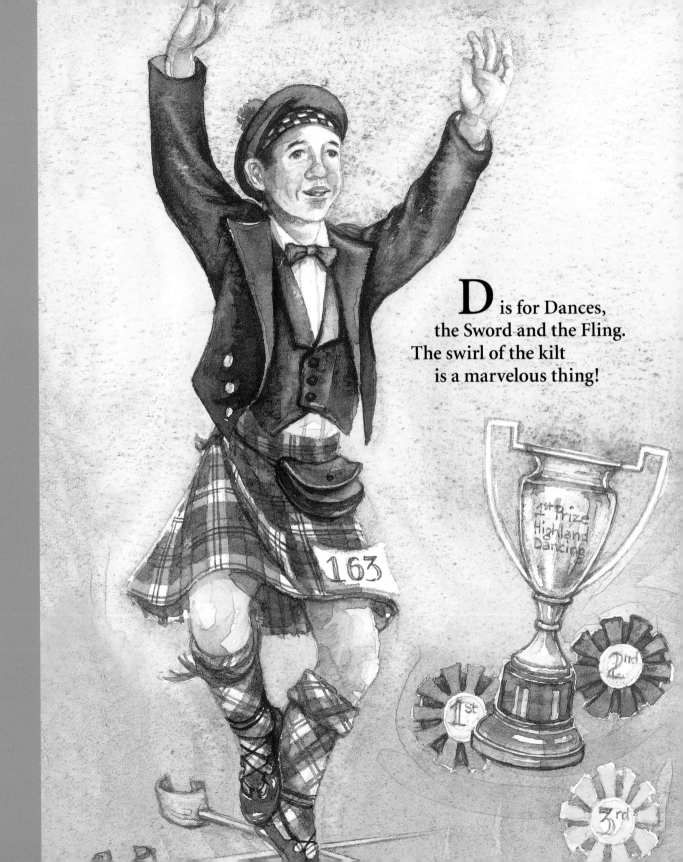

D is for Dances,
the Sword and the Fling.
The swirl of the kilt
is a marvelous thing!

All advance and retire to meet and pass on to the next 3 coming towards them

Dashing White Sergeant

At this stage in the dance 1st lady goes into the middle and dances 8 pas de basque steps

while the other 7 dancers make a circle and dance round 8 steps to the left and 8 steps back

Eightsome Reel

Edinburgh is Scotland's capital, a historic city of more than 400,000. The city's famous castle sits on a rock millions of years old where evidence of ancient people has been found.

In the center of town stand many buildings dating from the 1700s. Once a loch (lake), Princes Street Gardens is the setting for a thoughtful statue of Scotland's famous writer, Sir Walter Scott, looking at today's heavy traffic. The annual Edinburgh Festival of music, drama, opera, and dance draws hundreds of thousands of visitors from around the world.

Scottish doctors from the University of Edinburgh (founded in 1583) and from other Scottish Universities have made many contributions to medical science and continue to do so today.

Edinburgh is also home to the new Scottish Parliament building, opened in 2004. It is considered to be one of the most innovative building designs in the UK today.

E e

E is for Edinburgh,
great city of the North,
her ancient castle on a rock
beyond the Firth of Forth.

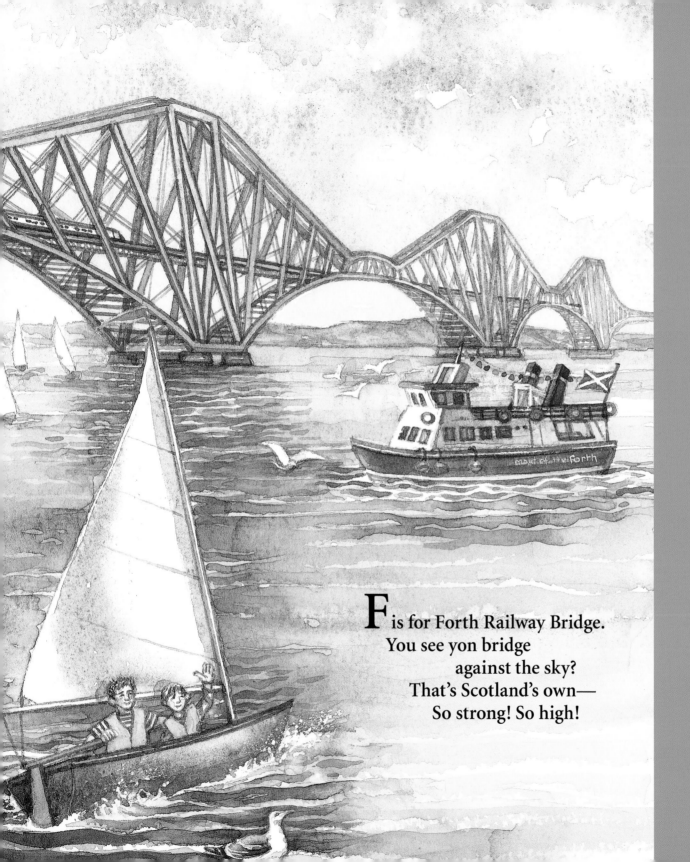

F is for Forth Railway Bridge.
You see yon bridge
  against the sky?
That's Scotland's own—
  So strong! So high!

The Forth Railway Bridge, the world's first major steel bridge, stretches for a mile and a half (2.4 km) across the Firth of Forth (estuary of the River Forth) just nine miles (14.5 km) from Scotland's capital city, Edinburgh. Designed by engineers John Fowler and Benjamin Baker and built by William Arrol's construction company between 1883 and 1890, the bridge was considered to be "one of the great feats of civilization." It is still looked upon as an engineering marvel, barely shaking in the highest winds. Today, two hundred trains cross the Forth Bridge daily, which stands out against Scottish skies with its famous paint, "Forth Bridge Red."

G's for Greyfriars Bobby,
the loyal Scottie dog,
who rested by his master's grave
in snow and rain and fog.

Bobby was a wee Skye terrier who holds a special place in the hearts of Scots, Edinburgh Scots in particular. He and his beloved master, John Gray, a police constable in Edinburgh during the mid-1850s, were best friends and known by many folk as they walked around town.

Sadly, Bobby's master died of tuberculosis in 1858 and was buried in the graveyard of Greyfriars Church. Bobby followed the procession to the cemetery and when everyone left, he stayed beside the grave. For fourteen years he remained there in all weathers, leaving only once a day to eat at a friend's when the one o'clock gun at Edinburgh Castle was fired. When he was sixteen or seventeen years old, Bobby's noble heart gave out and his gallant spirit went to join his master's.

If you visit Edinburgh's Greyfriars Church, you will find a beautiful sculpture of Bobby at the entrance to the churchyard.

Gg

H is for Haggis,
the sausage delicious!
High on the list
of tasty Scots dishes!

Is it true that the haggis is a shy, hairy beast inhabiting the lower slopes of the Scottish Highlands? No. It's a sausage!

Like many European countries hundreds of years ago, Scotland was poor. The rich enjoyed cuts of beef and mutton, while the poor made haggis from meat scraps. To make haggis they used a sheep's stomach to hold the precooked meat. The haggis is then boiled in water and served with mashed potatoes and rutabagas, known as "tatties and neeps."

On January 25th, Robert Burns's birthday, Scots everywhere hold Burns Suppers to celebrate the beloved poet. The crowning point is the tribute to his poem, "Address to a Haggis." While a piper pipes, a large haggis is escorted into the dining room where it is "addressed" by a speaker—yes, he talks to the haggis!

"Fair fa' your honest, sonsie face (Good luck to your honest, jolly face), Great chieftain o' the puddin-race!"

A poem written for a sausage? Ah, but such a sausage!

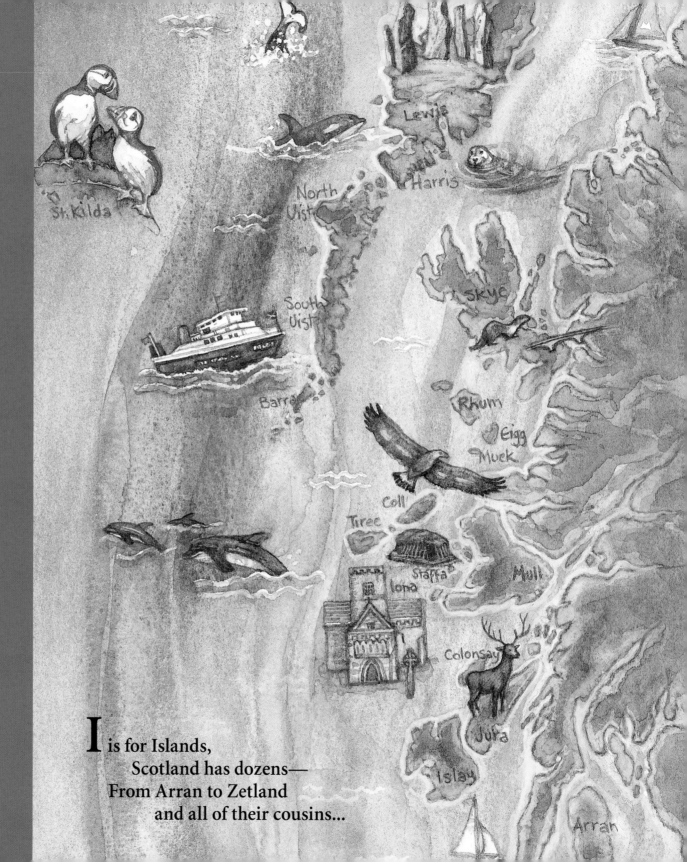

I i

Scotland is a small country with many islands along its coastline. Many of the islands are famous for different reasons. To learn more of Scotland's early times visit Iona, a small island where Saint Columba from Ireland established the first Christian settlement. Later, the monks of Iona produced the famous *Book of Kells*, giving us a rare picture of the Dark Ages. People also visit Fingal's Cave on Staffa where sounding waters inspired famed composer Felix Mendelssohn's Hebridean Overture.

Wildlife with whales, dolphins, eagles, and otters is everywhere. On St. Kilda, with the highest sea cliffs in the United Kingdom, lives the largest puffin colony in the UK. The island of Lewis has the Callanish Standing Stones, which are older than the Pyramids. Harris has the oldest rock in the world— Lewisian Gneiss. And if you go to the lovely Isle of Skye, you don't need to go "over the sea to Skye" in a boat. Now they have a bridge.

I is for Islands,
   Scotland has dozens—
From Arran to Zetland
   and all of their cousins...

The Jacobites were loyal supporters of King James II, who was banished by the Parliament because of religious and other differences. His supporters, angry that their king had been forced out, fought against the new king at the Battle of Sheriffmuir in 1715. It was a battle in which neither side won, but it was enough to drive King James to France, where he lived out the remainder of his life.

A rhyme says—
Some say that they won, and some say that we won
And some say that nane won at a', man.
But they ran and we ran and we ran and they ran
And they ran and we ran awa', man.

Thirty years later, King James's son, known as Bonnie Prince Charlie, went to Scotland to lead a second rebellion. Though he had raised a powerful army, mainly from the Highland Clans who fought fiercely at the Battle of Culloden, Charlie was also unsuccessful. But his struggle, his defeat, and his escape into the Highlands remain a part of Scotland's exciting history. He is remembered in song, the saddest being "Will Ye No Come Back Again?"

J is for Jacobite
(Jacobus is Latin for James).
There were seven kings
named James, James, James,
James, James, James—and James!

K is for Kilt,
the Scotsman's attire.
With fine sturdy legs,
he's a man to admire.

The kilt is the traditional garment worn by men. Women pipers and competitive Highland Dancers may also wear the kilt. Women in general wear a tartan skirt, which is not pleated like a kilt.

The kilt once was a long piece of tartan wool material (called a "plaid") which a Highlander wore every day. He gathered the lower part loosely into pleats, held in place with a belt; the upper part was swung around his shoulders and fixed with a brooch or pin. Old books tell us that the man had to lie down on the ground to do this! At night the plaid became a handy blanket. After many years the Scots cut the plaid in two, made the kilt out of the lower part and kept the rest for the upper body.

Buying a kilt, jacket, sporran, hose, and sgian dubh (a special dagger kept in the top of your sock) costs about $1000 today; the kilt alone about $500. The sporran is the purse that hangs from the waist. Kilts don't have pockets!

glengarry

tweed jacket

fur sporran

sock flashes
plain or tartan

balmoral

tie
plain or tartan

celtic leather sporran

sgian dubh
tucks into
top of sock

L's for the Monster
of gloomy Loch Ness
who's been spotted by many a Scot.
Critics say, "A monster? No way!"
But I say, "Oh really? Why not?"

Loch Ness is a deep freshwater lake located in the Scottish Highlands. In the 1800s, the Caledonian Canal joined the three lochs (Ness, Lochy, and Oich) forming a 60-mile (97-km) waterway from the Inverness area to Fort William. The murky waters of Loch Ness are deeper in places than the North Sea and have many underwater caves. Does some creature from the past still live there?

In the 1930s an English doctor visiting the Highlands took a photograph that rocked the country. The picture of a long-necked creature with a small head created an army of monster-seekers and many sightings were reported. The legend of the Loch Ness Monster grew. Local people called it Nessie. Nessie hit newspapers around the world and many people came to Scotland. Sonar findings reported something with a very large fin . . . but a more recent group using divers walking the loch floor found nothing. Still, it's easy to believe in Nessie when you stare across the waters of the loch on a dreary day . . . was that the flip of a tail we saw?

L_1

M m

Mary, born in 1542, was just a baby when her father King James V of Scotland died and she was crowned Queen of Scots. She had four dear friends, all called Mary, too. Mary Beaton, Mary Seton, Mary Livingstone, and Mary Fleming, who all stayed with her through her life as companions and attendants.

When Mary left for France at the age of five, the four Marys accompanied her to the court of King Henry II. At fifteen she married the young Dauphin Francis, heir to the French throne, but three years later Mary was a widow. She and her four Marys sailed to Scotland where the country was divided about her return. In England, Mary's cousin, Queen Elizabeth I, was uneasy because some believed Mary was also the lawful heir to the throne of England.

Those against Mary in Scotland eventually imprisoned her. She escaped to England, believing her cousin Elizabeth would defend her. She was wrong. After nineteen years in prison in stone-cold castles, Mary was executed at Fotheringay Castle in 1587. Her dear friends, the Marys, were spared and stayed with her to the last.

France 1549

M is for Mary, Queen of Scots.
who lived with hope and dread,
till one sad day at Fotheringay
she lost her royal head.

N is for Nature, that nurtures the Scot.
A daily reminder of what she has got.
The lochs and the glens, the deer on the hill—
Scots canna forget and indeed never will.

thistle

bluebell

primrose

wild rose

The Highlands are one of Europe's largest wilderness areas where Scots and their visitors love to hike, climb mountains, and watch wildlife. Wildflowers grow all over, and favorites are the thistle (symbol of Scotland), heather—both purple and the rarer white, and the fragrant little primrose, along with the vibrant bluebell that paints the spring woods. Scottish poet, Hugh MacDiarmid, touched the hearts of Scots everywhere when he wrote, "The little white rose of Scotland that smells sharp and sweet—and breaks the heart."

The ancient Caledonian Forest has all but disappeared, but aged trees from old forests continue to be important as they serve as homes and places of refuge for wild creatures. Scotland's unique countryside is protected by organizations like the Woodland Trust and the John Muir Trust. Scottish-born John Muir was an early conservationist who came to California in the late 1800s. He was responsible for preserving Yosemite and other national parks for us to enjoy today, and he was also a founder of the Sierra Club.

Scotland is a leader in the research and development of renewable energy sources like wind, wave, and tidal power. The dramatic Scottish landscape provides Scots with the opportunity to harness energy from the wind and the sea.

Nn

O is for Oatmeal,
"porridge" to the Scot.
Supped with milk, a pinch of salt—
and eaten while it's hot!

In the old days when a Scottish student left for the University he didn't go by train, car, bus, or plane. If he was lucky, he had a horse. If he was really poor, he walked carrying a pack with his belongings and some food. The food was usually dry oatmeal, which he could mix with stream water and a pinch of salt and cook in a small pot over a wood fire.

When oatmeal is cooked, the Scots call it porridge. For hundreds of years, porridge and herring were the staple foods for many Scots—both foods which we now know to be very nutritious. Long ago Scottish children went off to school after eating a bowl of "real" porridge, where the coarse oatmeal was soaked overnight to soften it for cooking.

But pity the children of long ago who never tasted a good oatmeal-and-raisin cookie!

There's an old Scots saying—"Keep your breath to cool your porridge"—meaning hold your tongue if you have nothing good to say, or it's a waste of time giving your opinion.

History tells us the Picts were "a mysterious race whose origin eludes us." Yet we know quite a lot about them. They were there when the Romans came to Scotland because the Romans gave them the name we still use—Picti, the "painted people." The writer Tacitus says they were a race of mixed tribes ("sturdy, stout-limbed, tawny-haired") who fought with iron claymores (swords), spears, and battleaxes. The Picts built tall, round towers called "brochs" with no window holes, in northern and northeastern Scotland. Some are still around.

In 83 AD the Picts were defeated by General Agricola at the Battle of Mons Graupius, but they kept on bothering the Romans—even after Hadrian built his wall! Finally the King of Scots, Kenneth MacAlpin, convinced the Picts to join him against the common enemy, the Vikings. In time they became part of the nation we know today. Scots, Celts, Danes, Norsemen, Anglo-Saxons—we are a nation of ancient immigrants.

P's for Picts, the "Painted Ones,"
who fought the Roman hordes
with strength and might and bitter fight,
and heavy-handed swords.

Quaich is pronounced "quake" with a "ccch" in the throat at the end! A quaich is an ancient Scottish drinking cup, small and shallow with a flat handle on either side. Its shape may have come from the scallop shells used in olden times as cups in parts of the Highlands. Some believe the original quaichs were used in ceremonies by the Druids to hold the blood of their sacrificial victims.

Long after the Druids, the same student who set out for University with his bag of oatmeal might also have carried his own wooden quaich. Some were formed by small flat pieces of wood bound together with leather. The simplest were hollowed out from one piece of wood and often had the owner's initials carved on one handle.

By the seventeenth century Scottish quaich-making had become a profession and quaichs were made of silver. Today silver and pewter quaichs are often given as gifts at weddings and christenings, or as welcome and farewell gifts for visitors. And if you want to toast someone with your quaich, say "Slainthe!" (pronounced "slanje") which means "Good health" in Gaelic.

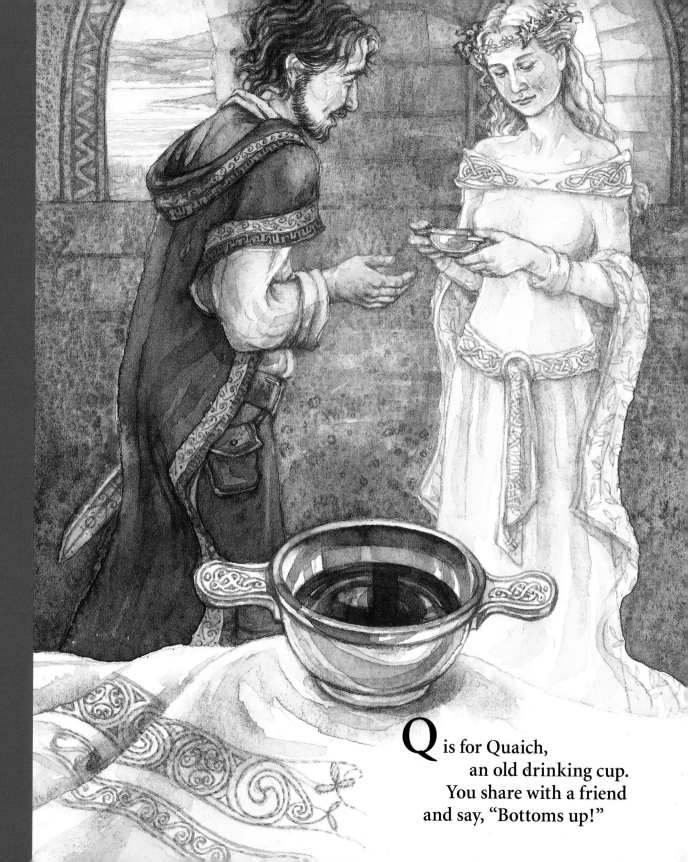

Q is for Quaich,
an old drinking cup.
You share with a friend
and say, "Bottoms up!"

Rr

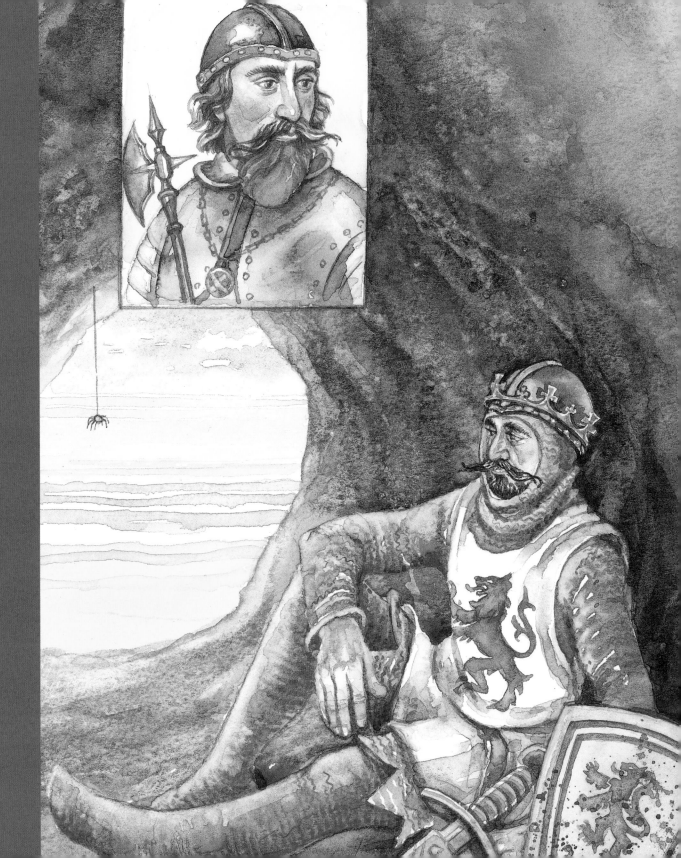

ROBERT THE BRUCE was the first king of an independent Scotland after the Battle of Bannockburn in 1314. Every Scots child knows the fable of Bruce and the spider. Bruce, hiding from enemies in a cave, watched a spider try to climb the wall. The spider fell back to the ground many times, but it kept on trying and finally reached the top. Bruce's own life was quite like the spider's.

ROBERT BURNS was a poet who spent many years as an unsuccessful farmer before the genius of his poetry was recognized. His works were mostly written in the dialect of Lowland Scotland ("Lallans"). He is considered to be Scotland's most famous poet.

ROBERT LOUIS STEVENSON left us the legacy of *Treasure Island, Kidnapped, Dr. Jekyll and Mr. Hyde,* and a dozen other books and delightful poems.

I have a little shadow that goes in and
*   out with me,*
And what can be the use of him is more
*   than I can see.*
He is very, very like me from the heels
*   up to the head;*
And I see him jump before me, when I
*   jump into my bed.*

—(from *A Child's Garden of Verses*)

To a Mouse
Wee, sleekit, cowrin, tim'rous beastie
O, what a panic's in thy breastie
Thou need na
wi bickering brattle!

R is for Roberts of whom there's a slew.
These three are more special so raise your cap to—
Robert the Bruce, King of Scots
Robert Burns, National Poet
Robert Louis Stevenson, beloved author.

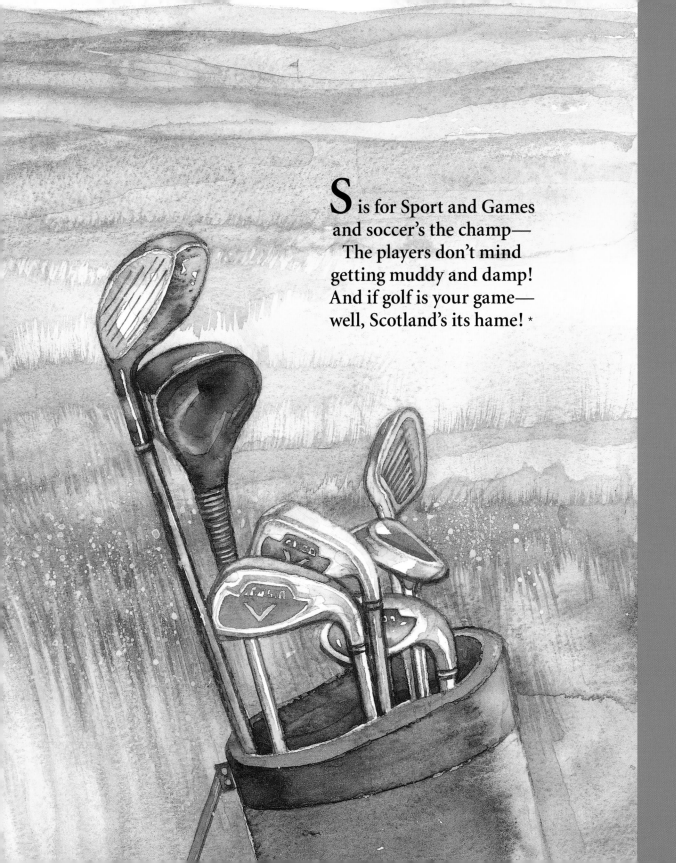

S is for Sport and Games
and soccer's the champ—
  The players don't mind
getting muddy and damp!
And if golf is your game—
  well, Scotland's its hame! *

Golf was born in Scotland and has been exported around the world. Shinty, a Highland game, is a wild kind of field hockey played with a curved stick called the camanachd. If you try it, wear a helmet. In the winter there's curling—where a heavy, polished stone is thrown down the ice, encouraged by players sweeping its path with brooms and yelling something that sounds very like "Soup!" But soccer is the most popular sport of all and is played by thousands of adults and children—and watched by millions.

Highland Games happen in towns all over Scotland in summer, with pipers and Highland dancers and competitive sports. These games started years ago when clans challenged each other to feats of strength and endurance. Tossing the caber is the most exciting, when kilted strongmen throw something like a telephone pole high in the air—hoping it will fall completely head over heels and not come back to hit them! If it falls all the way, that is a "twelve o'clock" and the winner!

* Scots for "home"

S

S

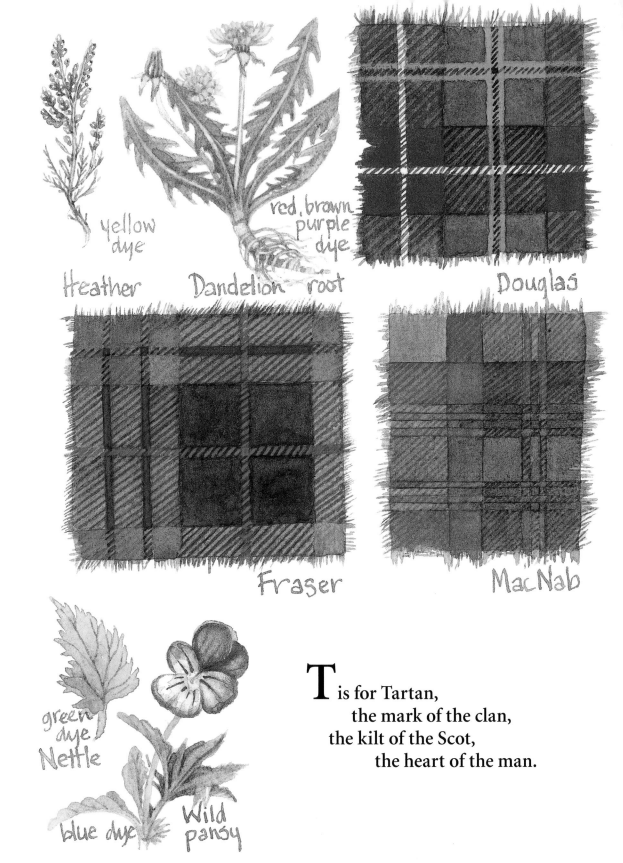

yellow
dye

red, brown
purple
dye

Heather

Dandelion root

Douglas

Fraser

MacNab

green
dye
Nettle

blue dye   Wild
             pansy

If you were asked to describe tartan to someone who had never seen it, what would you say? It's like different colored checks? Not really. Checks are made up of colored squares or oblongs. Tartans happen when lines of different colors cross each other on top of the basic checks, forming a more complicated pattern.

Tartans are hundreds of years old. They were woven by early Scots weavers using dyes from native plants to color the sheep's wool. Different weavers came up with different colors and designs so that the clan they belonged to might have a different tartan from the clan in the next glen. Your tartan then became very useful in a fight because you could recognize your friends—and your enemies. Today there are a couple of thousand named tartans on the list. Your name may be there!

T is for Tartan,
the mark of the clan,
the kilt of the Scot,
the heart of the man.

The name United Kingdom of Great Britain and Northern Ireland has been in use since 1927. It covers England, Scotland, Wales and Northern Ireland. The common language is English. Welsh is spoken by 26 percent of the people in Wales. A much smaller percentage of Scots in the Highlands and Islands speak Gaelic. Both languages are very ancient, although not alike.

In 1603 King James VI of Scotland became also King James I of England and moved himself and his Scots court south to London. About a hundred years later (1707) the English and Scottish parliaments were joined by the Treaty of Union after many disagreements. Much later and after bitter tribulations, it was decided that Northern Ireland would remain part of the United Kingdom.

This all means that if you are Scottish, English, Welsh, or Northern Irish when you get your passport, it will have the lion and the unicorn coat of arms on the cover and the words BRITISH PASSPORT United Kingdom of Great Britain and Northern Ireland stamped upon it. To the world we are "the UK"

St. Andrew + St. Patrick + St. George = Union Jack

Scotland · Northern Ireland · England · Wales ·

U is for United Kingdom—
Scotland and England,
Northern Ireland and Wales,
united they stand.
(UK in the mails.)

V is for Vole.
A Scots vole's not a water rat.
His blunt nose is much cuter.
His hairy coat and shorter tail,
the color of old pewter.

Many children know about Ratty from *The Wind in the Willows*, a classic tale by Kenneth Grahame, published back in 1908. Ratty isn't truly a water rat. He's a vole. And he has scores of cousins living in Scotland. A large vole population inhabits eight of the Orkney Islands as well as other areas. Some people say they may have lived in Scotland for about 4000 years and perhaps came as immigrants from as far away as the Continent. (Can't you see them setting out with their little suitcases?)

Scotland is also home to many other small animals, but the rarest are the pine marten, whose soft fur was prized long ago by kings, and the remarkable Scottish wildcat (sometimes called the Tiger of the Highlands). The Scottish wildcat is a critically endangered animal, much admired for its fierce independence and refusal to submit to any kind of human contact. These Tigers of the Highlands are quite similar to tabby house cats, but are much larger and have a very fierce appearance.

William Wallace was a Scottish patriot who vowed to free Scotland from the control of kings of England. With a small army, he defeated the large and better-equipped English army at the Battle of Stirling Bridge in 1297. A year later, however, the English king himself marched north with his troops and overpowered Wallace's smaller army at Falkirk.

Wallace escaped to France where the French king refused to help him and threw him into jail. He returned to Scotland a year later. In 1305 he was captured by his enemies and cruelly executed. The Wallace Monument outside Stirling reminds all Scots of William Wallace, a man of great courage and brave heart.

W is for William Wallace.
Wallace and his Scottish men
were strong and brave of spirit.
They saw a Scotland free and good
for children to inherit.

X is for Saint Andrew's Cross.
Scotland's flag is blue and white,
the Saltire is its name.
Saint Andrew is the Patron Saint
on whom the Scots lay claim.

More than a thousand years ago, old stories tell us that a Scottish king was almost conquered in battle. He looked up into the sky and saw a white cross against the blue. It was the cross of Saint Andrew, and the king vowed to make it the national flag of his homeland if the saint would help him win the battle. He won the battle and ever since then the cross of Saint Andrew has been the national flag of Scotland. Today Saint Andrew's flag (also called The Saltire), flies over many buildings in Scotland alongside the Union Jack (the flag of the UK). It is also flown at sporting events, and children know it as Saint Andrew's Cross.

Yule is an old word that the Vikings left us, and although it's not used much today, we still find expressions that our ancestors used in those far-off days. Yule is the way Scottish and English people pronounce the ancient Norse word "Jul," which means Christmas.

Today we may speak of the Yule log, which is the grand piece of tree that many people still cut down for their fireplaces at Christmas time. Yeel-day is our own Christmas day, December 25th.

In times gone by, Scottish children, as well as many others, had much simpler Christmases than we have today. They didn't receive lots of presents, and some might find just an orange in the toe of their stocking. The lucky ones might get a small toy, perhaps a doll, or a ball. Christmas vacation was called Yeel-play. If the family lived on a farm the farmer gave his workers a special Yule dinner. An ox killed for Christmas time was called a Yeel-mart. If you served cheese, it was called Yeel-kebbuck, and there was a special pudding dessert called Yule souwens, described as a "flummery." And after all the Yule feasting, there was always the last hole to which a man could stretch his belt—the Yule hole!

Yy

Y is for Yule or Yeel,
Christmas to you and me.
So put the turkey in the pot
and the star upon the tree!

Zetland is the old word for Shetland. The Shetland Islands are the northernmost part of Scotland, once known as Hjaltland (in Gaelic, Islands of the Cat People). Ancient peoples left us giant megaliths and Iron Age dwellings there. Vikings settled in Shetland and some local folks still speak Norn, a unique version of Scots with a Scandinavian touch.

Sixteen of the islands and skerries (small rocky islands) are inhabited. The largest is called Mainland (population 17,550). Historically the islands are known for fishing, sheep-farming, knitting, and weaving—and remember Shetland sheepdogs and ponies! Tiny Fair Isle was always famous for knitwear with designs that sing of Norway, and in the Out Skerries you can see the Northern Lights. More recently, the Shetland Islands are known for The North Sea Sullom Voe Terminal, one of the largest oil and gas terminals in Europe.

Still today on the last Tuesday of January, the town of Lerwick goes crazy with the "Up-Helly-Aa" celebrations of ancient times. Hundreds of people work all year to organize these reenactments until finally everyone sees the year's chosen "Guizer Jarl"—the leader of the festival. The Jarl is dragged on his ship—which took three months to build—and after the Jarl disembarks, flaming torches are tossed on deck, the ship is burned, and everyone sings "The Norseman's Home."

Zz

Up Helly Aa

Mousa Broch

Fair Isle knitting

Z is for Zetland,
The northernmost isles—
we won them from Norway
with warfare and wiles.

Eve Begley Kiehm

Eve Begley Kiehm was born in Bridge of Allan, Scotland, in a house across the fields from Stirling Castle. She has a master's degree in Scottish History and Literature from Glasgow University and an early childhood education certification from the University of Toronto. In addition to *B is for Bagpipes*, her published books about Scotland have included a young adult historical adventure novel set in the 11th century, and an adult non-fiction book. She regularly visits Scotland, but makes her home in the San Diego area with her family.

Alexa Rutherford

Alexa Rutherford is a Scottish illustrator having studied at Duncan of Jordanstone College of Art, Dundee, Scotland. She has 35 years of experience in children's book illustration in the UK. A series of more than 30 "Kelpie" book covers on Scottish children's literature led to US commissions when *Quest for a Maid* was re-used by an American publisher.

B is for Bagpipes is her first book for Sleeping Bear Press, and she is delighted to have the opportunity to show her country's history and culture. Alexa lives in Edinburgh with her husband. She has two grown children. To see more of her work go to www.alexarutherford.co.uk.